Interview Hacks

How to Persuasively Work ANY Interview
with Proven Tactics and Strategies

Why Read This Book?

This book will not guarantee you a job.

But it will absolutely increase your chances. If you're looking for a long book with all the technicalities involved in the interview process, how to write a resume and good CV, or how to answer certain types of questions, this might not be the right book for you.

Yes, at the end of the book we will be going through some practical things like common interview questions, persuasive body language and other things that may seem like common sense (though we are too quick to gloss over these foundational principles).

But the main purpose of this short book, however, is to show you the unstoppable mindset you need to have that draws people – including employers – irresistibly to you. The actionable parts like what to dress, how to answer your questions, etc. are all infinitely secondary. If you can master this mindset, you can nail the interview, not just with your potential employer, but in all of life.

All of life is a series of interviews. First impressions are interviews. People scrolling through your social media is an interview. Every single day that you meet somebody new (or even a familiar), you're submitting yourself to an interview process as they observe you and ask, "Do I like this person?", "What type of person is this?", "Can I trust this person?", "What's unique about this person?".

This is what separates successful people and unsuccessful people.

Successful people know that all of life is an interview, and they've mastered this interview mindset. That is the true interview hack. You can spend hours researching the right interview questions, perfecting your resume, and practicing your speeches. But unless you completely commit yourself to become an expert in this mindset, you'll be wasting your time.

Too harsh? Well, this is the real world. I'm writing this short book for your sake and I guarantee, if you start to follow these principles, you'll find yourself crushing it not only in job interviews, but in life.

Author's Note

Before we dive in, I wanted to share a little bit about myself. My name is Henry.

But that doesn't really matter, does it?

You didn't buy this book (or you're not thinking of buying this book) because you cared to know who I was. You're reading this book to learn what you can get out of it, what value it can give you.

And that's okay. I'm not offended.

Though I used to be. But when I learned how not to be, when I learned how to be unoffendable, I learned the mindset that opened up hundreds of doors for me.

I grew up as a shy kid. I didn't have many friends and I wanted desperately to fit in. My social skills were non-existent and I wasn't the best -looking kid on the block. I did everything I could to get people to like me, to accept me, to include me. I talked the way they did, I laughed at the things they laughed at. I did everything I could not to be different; not to stand out. I did everything in my power to make a good impression, hoping that I would appear likeable.

That didn't get me anywhere. The more I tried to fit in, the more I was excluded. The more I tried to get them to like me, the more I drove people away.

Things only got worse when I began to apply for jobs in the corporate world. I double majored in marketing and finance, with a minor in accounting. I got my MBA and then another Master's degree in business administration. With this resume, I couldn't imagine any company not wanting to hire me. I sent in my applications and went to hundreds of interviews.
I didn't hear back from any of them.
Not a single phone call.

It was then, at the lowest point in my life, I knew I had to change. Everything I thought I knew about the real world was wrong. Your college degree promises you nothing. Absolutely nothing. A good education could not promise you success. Only one thing can: the interview mindset. I call it my interview hack.

After my failure, I became obsessed with learning how to get people to like me. It sounds sad, but I went about this very methodologically. I took notes. I studied human psychology and followed case studies. I read hundreds of books and went to dozens of seminars.

And what I learned is infinitely more valuable than what you'll ever learn in college, I can guarantee you that.

Because when you realize that all of life is an interview and you become an expert on how to navigate these interviews skillfully, whether first impressions, social media, or job interviews, you'll never worry if people will hire you or not.
Or at least people won't think that you ever worry.
And that's why they'll want to hire you.

Table of Contents:

Acknowledgements

Thank you, Mary, for telling me to take the next step. Without your nagging, I'd still be reading comics on the playground with no ambition.

I still love comics.

"The interview never becomes larger than the person being interviewed."

Ken Burns

Chapter 1

The Interview Mindset

This chapter will serve as the foundation upon which the subsequent chapters are built. While most books dedicate hundreds of pages to the practical tips in the last few chapters, they will serve no purpose if not accompanied with the interview mindset.

Why is the interview mindset so important? Simply because we live out who we believe we are. We act out our self-given identity. And if you don't see yourself as the most competent person that should be hired, there is no way you will act the part.

So what is the interview mindset? It is simply the mindset that seeks nothing from people and only for people.

Let me explain.

It is only when you don't seek anything from people, be it their attention, their adoration, their acceptance. It's only when you don't need that will you even have a chance of earning it. People are repelled by neediness, perhaps because they see themselves in it. But when they come across somebody who is confident, secure, and not needing of people's adoration, people begin to notice.

And then to seal the deal, when this confident person is not only self-sufficient, but seeks the good of others, people cannot help but be drawn in. Why? Because this is counterintuitive. It's not normal. But when you learn how to master this mindset, you learn how to win people.

The reality is, people like, trust, hire, and follow people that:
1.	They like and admire
2.	Like and are interested in them
3.	Are similar to them

We're going to break this mindset into five principles or the five pillars that create this mindset.

It is crucial that you develop these mental habits overtime to master life's interviews.

Principle #1: Be the Leader

Be the leader. Even when you're not. Display authority, even when you don't have it. The truth is, you don't need an actual position of leadership to give off a sense of influence. Not at all. Leadership happens when you come across as somebody who knows what he or she's doing. Somebody with an established sense of self and purpose.

In the interview room, this looks like you displaying confidence in yourself. It means walking into the interview with the mindset that your time is limited and valuable, you have other options (or will have them), you know that this company desperately needs to fill this position, and you'll give them some time to sell it to you.

What you enter the room with that mindset, your responses and your attitude will inevitably change. It will be completely different than walking into the room, fingers-crossed, palms sweaty, hoping they'll like you and your resume out of the other 200 applicants.

No.

The first step is to tell yourself that you do not need this job. You'll find other jobs. You'll find other ways. But your life does not depend on this job, this interview, or this hiring manager. You refuse to give them that power over you.

A CEO or military general will never walk into a conference room, hoping the conversation will go well and people will like them. They have too many other things to care about and their time is limited. Their existence, security, reputation, or self-worth simply is not be threatened by anybody in that room and everybody knows that when they walk in.

At this point you might argue: But they already have a job. They already have respect. They are already in that position of leadership so of course it's easy for them.

And that's where you're wrong. Because successful CEO's, generals, and leaders all had this mindset long before they ever got their position. In fact, it was this very mindset that got them there.

All this to say that you must wake up every morning with a clear sense of who you are and what your purpose is. If you don't know what it is, then find it. Write it out on paper. You need to know your mission in this world and your unique contribution that only YOU can offer. Not Bill Gates, not Steve Jobs, not your hiring manager, not your next-door neighbor, but you. What skill, personality trait, talent, or experience that you uniquely have that sets you apart.

And then ask yourself this question: With my uniqueness, what difference in this world am I called to make?

It could be that you have a keen eye for imagining designs and ideas that have yet to be created, that the world needs.

It could be that you're a great organizer and you're called to lead groups of people to new endeavors.
Whatever it is, don't do anything until you answer this question.

When you answer this question and give your life to it, leadership begins. When you have embraced this mindset, you'll be able to walk into any room as a leader with a defined mission and defined personal values. A mission and values that you believe with complete conviction are necessary and beneficial for this world and for everybody in it. That includes your hiring manager, when you walk in for your interview.

And when you've fully embraced this vision of yourself and of your life, you will start to become somebody who doesn't need anything from others, at all. And that's the beginning of leadership.

"The question isn't who is going to let me; it's who is going to stop me." Ayn Rand.

Principle #2: Be Knowledgeable

"Ipsa Scientia Potestas Est
Knowledge itself is power."
Sir Francis Bacon

To be a true leader and true master of interviews and life, you must be knowledgeable. There is no way around this. You must commit yourself to a lifelong quest of learning and growing in your knowledge.

You can tell immediately who the leader in the room is by seeing who everybody naturally turns to when a question is asked. Even if they don't have the official position of authority. Why? Because they're the most likely to know the answer. And those who know are those we follow.

Every great leader in history has been a reader of books, journals, magazines, and nowadays, blogs and web articles. It is only through a cultivated habit of learning that you begin to get a grasp on how everything connects in this world, from economics, to political science, to stock market, to human psychology, biology, and even chemistry.

This isn't to say that you need to be an expert on every subject. That would be impossible and a futile endeavor. Yet to at least have a framework on these different arenas and sectors of life and society is to grant you access to the top 10% of people who stand out above the crowd. The 10% of people who are likely to be followed.

There is a reason for this.

The sad reality is too often our educational systems are flawed in that we are encouraged to pursue academics over education. We are rewarded for our test-taking skills, rather than our skill of creativity and success.

Most of society is trained to live by the system and to strive for the things the system encourages: Get straight A's, study for long hours to pass exams (even if you don't grasp the material), partake in activities purely to buff up your resume, go to college and get a degree, study for the sake of studying and passing, get an internship position or two, and then start applying for jobs. Hopefully you land a job and you can settle into a comfortable life.

This creates a societal tunnel-vision. We have sacrificed education for systematic academics that are only rewarded if we follow the system and pattern that has been laid out for us.

This type of learning does not create leaders.

True leaders move beyond that, whether intentionally or unintentionally, and seek to learn how the world works. They seek to learn how people work and how culture works.

This happens through education, not academics. This happens through personal study driven by passion, not punishment. This is motivated by curiosity, not curriculums.

And if you develop and master this habit of constantly learning not for the sake of grades, but for the sake of growth, then you will have a break through. Not many people make it through this. Too many are content with playing the academic game, doing whatever it takes to get good grades, to get good resumes, to get mediocre jobs, and submit themselves to whatever the system, hiring managers, and organizations want from them, for the rest of their lives.

You must break free from this.

It is when you develop this habit, you will be a leader and be somebody worth following. You will seek to create, not simply to conform. You will be defined by a passion to sail the seas, rather than the fear of rocking the proverbial boat.

When you master these two principles we've talked about so far, you will become a person that people esteem; that people like; that people admire. That is the first step to leadership and that is the first step to the interview mindset.

Principle #3: Be an Expert Affirmer

The natural disposition of a person is to live a self-absorbed life. It's a sad reality, but as I mentioned in the first few pages of this book, that's how I lived.
As human beings, we are all naturally self-centered and overly self-conscious. Call it psychology, or evolutionary traits, or sin, or whatever worldview you come from, we cannot deny this fact. But we can use it to our advantage.

Remember, the three types of people that people like?
1.   People that they like

2.   People that like them

3.   People that are like them.

The first two principles (be a leader and be knowledge) set you up to be the first type of person. People like leaders. People follow those that are not needy or dependent on others. And people admire those that are knowledgeable.

To be the second type of person is the goal of this principle.

If you want somebody to like you and trust you, you must be their biggest affirmer. You must be their biggest fan. You must exhibit genuine curiosity in their life, their hobbies, their passions, their struggles, and their fears. You must authentically want to know more about them and they will know if you are authentic or not.

And the only way to genuinely show border-line obsessive interest in somebody is to be a person that does not need anything from them. In other words: get over yourself. You simply cannot be genuinely interested in their life if you are desperately dependant and in need of their approval or affirmation.

You must resolve firmly that you do NOT need this person to like you, whether it's a girl or boy you're romantically interested in, or if it's a hiring manager, or a new classmate. You must find this sense of self-approval elsewhere. You must be self-secured in your own sense of self-worth, in your values, and in your unique mission.

Then, and only then, can you devote yourself to being interested in other people. And believe me, these type of people are rare. But I'm sure you know that.

Let's bring this back to the interview room.

If you walk in to the interview room, not nervous about getting this job because you don't need this job. Not wringing your hands, nervously hoping you'll be accepted. Instead, if you walk in, confident in your purpose, with the mindset that you are giving them the opportunity to hire you, you are freed to act naturally. You will be more relaxed and be an expert affirmer. Your job now is to do your best to naturally affirm whatever you can about them, making them feel valuable and liked. They will remember this.

Whenever you have conversations with new people, who are the people you remember to this day? People that complimented you. People that said nice things about you and affirmed you. Even if it was as simple as them saying they liked your shoes or your shirt. Do you remember how you immediately felt about those people? You liked them.

If you were a hiring manager, conducting hundreds of interviews with hundreds of people a day, who would you remember? Those that made you feel affirmed and special.

You can comment on how you like their shirt, or if the topic arises, you can casually start a conversation about their hobbies or their life. Only people with this right mindset can ever hope to accomplish this naturally, and it's these people that get hired to become leaders.

Principle #4: Get in Their World

This principle deals with the last type of person that people like: People that are like them. If you've ever been a new place, whether traveling, or a new school, or a new job, who do you gravitate towards?

People that are like you.

It could be anything from how they dress, their ethnicity, their personality, etc. And when you start to get to know people more, you're drawn even closer to those who share similar interests as you, whether hobbies, or religion, or past experiences.

Those with the interview mindset know this well and will do everything to make these connections. When these connections are made, hiring managers are 50% more likely to remember your name.

Obviously you're going to want to do this naturally. In other words, this does not call for an awkward, "Hi I'm Henry, WHAT DO YOU LIKE TO DO?" Experts at this try to naturally thread this into a conversation.

"You've got an interesting last name. May I ask where it's from?"

And since everybody loves taking about themselves, they'll answer. At this point, you can say:

"Oh, it's French? I went to France 2 years ago, it was beautiful!"

Or if you didn't go to France,

"Oh that's lovely! I have a friend from France and she's always raving about _____."

If you're lucky, this might spark further conversation. You might not be able to make connections easily, but this is a skill you must develop. You must train your eyes to look for things that could create conversations.

What does their coffee mug say?

What does their University Diploma say? What did they study?

What does their tattoo mean?

If you can establish a connection with them (or anybody in life), this will put you in a different league all together. You'll realize that this skill will be directly increased by how skilled you are in principle 2.

Principle #5: Be Reserved

This fifth and last principle might seem a bit out of place, but there is a good reason for this component of this mindset. Bluntly stated, people admire those who never show all of their cards. I don't mean in a shady, suspicious kind of way causing people to question whether or not you're a murderer.

Rather, I mean to suggest to act in such a way that you always have things under control, even when you don't. Always appear to have an alternative plan, for the sake of others. Why? Because people look to leaders who have answers, even when the leaders don't have answer.

This is a common human characteristic and it's often exhibited in the movies we watch. All of the leaders that are portrayed as respected are also portrayed as slightly mysterious and reserved, as if they always know something we don't and we can trust them for that. Just a few examples of this are Dumbledore, Professor Xavier, Yoda, Batman, Jack Sparrow, Jesus, Rick Grimes

(Walking Dead), Oliver Queen (Arrow). We can go on forever.

Chapter 2

Practical Tips for Preparation

Now that we've talked about the interview mindset (which, like all habits, will not form overnight), we can proceed to the lesser important tips. These tips are helpful, but only if done from the right mindset. Nonetheless, we shall explore them.

Often, it so happens that when we see a corporation publishing an advertisement in the newspaper, we assume that it's a big deal to apply and successfully get into the said corporation.

However, you must keep in mind the fact that it was the corporation that published the need for an employee and not the other way around. If they were not in desperate need of someone skilled, they would not have hit the papers.

The first hurdle has thus been taken care of. You need to remember that they need you and not the other way around. Yes, you too have the need for a job that pays, but it is their need that overshadows yours. As soon as you read the published call for an interview, you must mentally prepare yourself to grab the opportunity with both your hands.

As opposed to just concentrating on how you will profit by having the employment, you need to understand that occupations are truly about offering some incentive to an association and their clients.

Going into an interview with the outlook of how you will offer some incentive to the association allows you to approach the job from an entirely different perspective altogether.

Many individuals, with incessant health conditions, usually suffer from a lack of self-confidence due to their physical confinements. And when money related stress and unpaid bills are added to the blend, the result is an increased mental strain. The more desperate you are for work, the more scared you may look and become during the interview. You may feel like you need to request and even beg for something that you need, as opposed to offering the utilization of your talents.

Take a gander at work as a fair deal. In this deal, you trade your skills and potential for wages, in return for fair wages and an opportunity to learn something new. That sounds more reasonable than simply looking at the situation as being you hunting for a job and desperately trying to go through the interview to get it. You will be amazed that this newly discovered certainty that you have gained, just by reaching this mere conclusion, will propel your self-confidence.

Organizations are populated by individuals. These individuals have characters that are regularly attached to their organization culture. By doing a touch of research in advance, you can address the vital components of their corporate character. This quickly puts you ahead of other people who are just searching for a job.

Noteworthy Answers

The most common question that is asked at any job interview is "Why do you need this job?" Now, you can go either way in answering this question; honest or otherwise. Numerous people will drift on about how they need the cash to pay past due bills, need better health advantages or even discuss how close the workplace is to their home.

If you want to launch into a speech of how unpaid bills have been surmounting for months and how much of a financial crunch you are in, you will be playing the game the honest way, the straight way. Despite there being truth present in this answer, it won't really cut it. The employer is not interested in the sob story concerning why you are looking for a job. They are more concerned about how you could benefit the prospective employer, or what's in it for them.

Another annoying yet important question commonly asked by employers is, "What are your strengths?" Now, the obvious way to answer this would be to list all the strong points of not just your academics, but also of your personality. However, everyone else will be doing the same thing. Instead, focus more on your personal traits than those already mentioned in your resume. By choosing to do so, you are showing the employer the side of you that has not been displayed elsewhere. When you prove to your employer that you are more than just your grades and points, it instills a faith towards you in them.

Similarly, a lot of interviewers ask you about your weaknesses. They aren't really interested to know where you lack. The main intention behind asking this question is to know whether you are self-aware of your weaknesses or not. After being asked about your weaknesses, if you end up answering with "none," there is a good chance of you being disqualified then and there. Always be honest while facing this question because, after you are hired, your employers are going to come across your weak points anyway. So, it is better if they are prepared to deal with them, rather than surprising them and facing the backlash. Hence, it is always better to be honest than sorry. It also shows them that you are aware of your weaknesses as well as your strengths and that's important in the workplace.

A good CV

A CV is what represents you when you are seeking a job. It talks about you in a manner you wouldn't be able to explain in a personal interview. It is the prima facie evidence of your credentials and displays your potential to those who are in a position to award you a job. It is of paramount importance that you start working towards building a good CV right from your student days. Interning at good places, presenting papers on your subjects and working under experienced and renowned people from your field, are some of the very significant things that a competitive CV should contain.

A CV is an official proof that you possess the requisite capabilities to perform the said job. There are some basic things that should be taken care of during the preparation of a CV.

The course that you are pursuing should be consistent with the job that you are seeking. Choose a course that is inclusive of as many degrees as possible. At times, the presence of an integrated degree scores you brownie points, despite the fact that the integrated individual degrees might not give you a chance of getting you a job, when looked at in isolation.

A good CV also has recommendations from all the right places. It is desirable that you intern and gain experience from people and places that matter and that stand up to the scrutiny of people who may be interviewing you. If those established in the arena claim you are good at your work, it counts a great deal when you go out on the hunt for jobs. With their backing, you stand more chance of getting the job you want.

It is also important to use a clean and legible format. Whoever said looks don't matter never saw a badly formatted resume. A resume is supposed to create a first impression and a bad format and wrong fonts can really mar your chances to even sit for an interview, let alone land the job. Make your resume stand out.

Be honest

A very important thing that needs to be kept in mind while updating your resume is that lying will eventually come back to bite your precious posterior in the long run. Companies often have a policy of running background checks on candidates applying for a job with them. If they find something that's misleading or even slightly unreliable, they will do more than just reject your application. Most companies have a database of lying candidates, which gets shared through the entire regime of companies. The habitual offenders are blacklisted there and then and any company will tend to enter your name in the database to know whether you have a history of lying in your resumes. Once your name enters the mentioned database, it's in there forever. So, being dishonest in your resume will not only quash your current job, but also dampen any future opportunities you might have.

Proofreading is a must

Before you submit your resume for a future employer to look at, make sure at least two people go through it for the purpose of finding any factual or grammatical errors. A simple typo may ruin your chances to land an interview - for it displays casual approach on your part.

Do your homework

It is not enough that a good CV is produced. It needs to be followed up by a good amount of research and background checks on the place you are applying for a job. Getting to know about their history, establishment of facts, merger policies and other relevant information about them can come in handy when you are called in for an interview. Being well versed with the company and their nature of work makes you stand in a good light and sends a message to the interviewer that says you are really interested in working with them. It elevates your chances of getting selected when you show them how much you know about them and their work.

The D-Day

An interview is supposed to test you on the practical grounds of the game and recheck the claims you made in the submitted resume. It is of primary importance that your interview goes well.

First off, dress up properly for the interview. Formals work most of the time. If any specific color or dress code has been asked for, follow it to the letter. Do not mismatch your ties and socks and absolutely do not opt for bright and garish colors that would blind the butterflies. It is preferred that you opt for somber colored suits to bring out a look of professionalism. Also, take care of your personal hygiene before walking into the interview room. Overgrown beard, dirty nails and filthily running noses are corporate turn-offs. They not only score against you, but also reflect your personality in society. Someone who's arrived groomed and suited up like a gentleman is most likely to be favored over someone who couldn't find time for some self-improvisation.

Make sure your posture while walking in, sitting and getting up is, if not militarily perfect, at least not worthy of receiving a cringe from the judges. Postures illustrate your approach towards things in general. A laid back sitting posture gives off an aura of disrespect, while one of rapt attention gives off positive vibes.

Another very vital part of interviews is how you converse. The way you choose to speak speaks a lot about you. Use lively and formal language like – "I'd like to explore this opportunity'' and not "Yeah, it'd be good if I worked with you."

While talking to those conducting your interview, look them in the eye and talk confidently. Your tone should indicate that you are aware of your abilities and confident about them. Guard against too much gaudiness and exaggeration when you are asked to describe yourself. Interviews usually start with a warming up question like "tell us about yourself."

Ensure briefness and quickness in answering this sort of question. They are supposed to make you feel comfortable before the interview continues on to more technical questions and discussions. Limit the timing of the answer to such questions to 30 seconds. A short yet inclusive description of your hobbies and qualifications needs to be presented. No one's going to ask further questions on this answer because it's just a warming up process.

Admit your faults

If, during the interview, you are caught off guard by a question that you have no clue about, it is detrimental to your chances to go on and on beating around the bush than admitting that you don't know the answer. Bluffing attempts never impress the interview conductors. However, an honest "I'm sorry sir, I have absolutely no idea whatsoever." might just work in your favor. And it also adds a bonus to your score if you politely ask the conductor the right answer after you've admitted your incompetency.

Companies reward those who like to learn and dissent those who just try to faff their way out of a difficult situation or just blabber about something they don't know the answer to. Your inquisitiveness gets you an edge over those who didn't bother to answer and sulked because they weren't good at it.

Skill-sets

An employer always looks forward to hiring those who have a basic set of skills. Some of them are – logical thinking, communication abilities, technical accuracy and interpersonal skills.
Logical thinking includes the capability of the human mind to arrive at conclusions and take decisions based on the power of reason. Inductive, deductive and adductive reasoning capabilities constitute a basic logic set. Not everyone is capable of thinking logically in adverse situations and unforeseen circumstances. The higher the

degree of logic found in a potential employee, the greater his chances of getting hired.

Communication skills are requisite to survive a job interview. If you are not able to convey your problems to your employer and fellow employees in a convenient manner, then you are most likely not the right person for the job. An employer-employee relationship involves the reporting of activities to the employer. Going behind the employer's back or not telling him about an important fact that might affect the company is considered to demonstrate a lack of communication skills.

Technical accuracy is a very basic requirement. You may be a great people person and you may have an I.Q. of over 130, but if you fail at getting the technical bolts and nuts right, you are pruned from the beginning. Being technically good implies getting your fundamentals are strong.

A job at a bank may involve being a wizard at accounting and mathematical mumbo jumbo. Or a law firm may need you to be well versed with the state laws or the constitution.

A job is more than about just doing work and getting paid. It has an office and several other employees working alongside you. It becomes an unspoken rule to work not just for the employer, but also with your fellow comrades. An interviewer will be curious to test your social skills by asking about your friend circle or how you spend your leisure hours. Hypothetical questions based on imagined scenarios should also be expected.

Internships

Internships are a great way to get in touch with a company even before you start thinking of working for them. An internship not only gets you referrals, but also adjusts you to the work environment and the culture of it. You get to know fellow employees and the nature of their work.

This helps you in deciding if you want to work there or not. Interning at a place can be done during college vacations or part time if your college and workplace allow it. Start off by volunteering for the work and eventually, when they start noticing your work, they might just pay you for it. Volunteering displays your commitment to the work. Companies look into their internship box for future recruitments. It is a cost-effective method of ensuring the continuance of providing employment. Interns are preferred over random applicants any day.

Personal touch

If possible, get in touch with the HR of the company you are interested in working for. Although it sounds negative, you can try using your personal relationship with them to land a job in the company. One shouldn't be ashamed of accepting a job acquired through personal contacts. After all, this is Darwinism at its best. The fact that you are known to the people hiring you also gives you an edge in the interview process, but don't take it for granted.

Right Approach

Impress the interviewer with your common sense and cool approach. Many interviewers try to catch the candidate off guard with unconventional questions and scenarios. A hypothetical situation is given and the candidate is asked to answer what he'd do if placed in this situation. A cool and humorous approach to answering such questions helps your chances. Do not panic and let the suddenness of the question boggle you. Apply a pinch of common sense and you will soar through them.

Take the first step

If you are employed on a trial basis or if you are an intern - ask for work. It goes against your interests that you sit at a desk all day surfing the Internet because no work has been assigned to you. Speak up and ask for work. If necessary, nag your boss into giving you some work and let him know you don't want to sit idle and useless. Always look like you are busy with something.

Find a job that interests you

Do not go looking for fat paychecks jobs if you are not sure you'd like to devote your time to the job in hand. Having skills for a job is different from having the mind for it. If you are not someone who likes to do a mundane desk job, then don't apply for one. Instead, search for jobs that inspire you to think outside the cubicle.

Negotiations

The real talk of your interview happens usually at the end of it. This is when you are asked about the remuneration part of the job. The interviewer may just give you ball park figures. If the interviewer is simply conveying to you the amount that you should be expecting, you have no choice but to accept it or leave it. This happens with jobs whose advertisements have explicitly mentioned the exact compensation you will be getting. There is a hint of "no negotiation" in this ad and you should have noticed it. It therefore becomes unprofessional to even attempt a negotiation in such a scenario.

However, if the job's advertisement or notice had no such mention of remuneration, it is implied that they are willing to engage you in a negotiation over it. Here are some of the tips you must keep in mind while negotiating:

Keep in mind your skills, achievements and experience before blurting out an amount. Your resume must justify the amount you are quoting. If you quote something obscenely higher than you obviously seem to deserve, it may put off the interviewer. Likewise, if you quote too low a remuneration, it will not only be disadvantageous for you, but you will also come across as foolish to those sitting across the table.

Never quote your compensation amount all on your own. Always be polite and ask the interviewer about the price they think you deserve based on your resume and performance in the interview.

If you have been told a figure that you are not happy with, express it in a manner that does not show disappointment or dissent.

Tell the interviewers about your past jobs and how much you were paid. You can sometimes choose to be a bit liberal regarding this figure since the crosschecking salary figures of candidates in their previous jobs is not a regular practice. However, play this game with caution as, if discovered, it may lead you to get blacklisted.

Always ask if the salary that is being offered comes with tax-cuts or without them. Usually, the salary that's written into your employment agreement is more than you actually get. This is because of various taxes, 401(k), and other similar cuts. Make sure you know exactly what you are getting before you commit.

Chapter 3

Using Body Language

Welcome to the final chapter of this book. In this chapter, we will discuss how you can effectively use your body language and its relevance in job interviews. You speak with more than just words. Your body speaks while you are not paying much attention and you unintentionally end up saying a lot about your inner emotions through your body. Though it is purely unintentional in nature, you can learn to master it, so as to use it to your own advantage in job interviews.

Facial Expressions

Your face says a lot about you. Without treading into the unsafe field of first impressions, your face is your entire profile in an interview. It is the first thing people notice when you walk into the room. Your mind, your intellect, your wit, your sense of humor; all come secondary to the onlookers' minds. It is your face that leads everything else.

Droopy eyes clearly indicate that the person is not interested in what is in front of him. It may, at times, even be offensive to some people. On the other hand, attentive and alert eyes signify that you are genuinely taking interest what the other person has to say. However, popping out eyes is a sign towards overacting. If a person's eyes follows the speaker's hand movement, blink at the right time intervals and do not have eye-sand in them, it leaves behind a good impression on the speaker.

Watch your mouth. Literally! The way you position your lips in an interview is vital towards indicating what mood you are in! If you have an open mouth, it shows that either you are dumbfounded by the conversation's contents or you are simply sitting there not listening to whatever's being said. On the other hand, if you use your lips to occasionally smile a little, it may encourage the interviewer to do more of what they are doing.

If you are twitching your lips, it indicates that you are under a bit of stress. Lip twitching has always been associated with nervousness. If you twitch your lips in a job interview, your chances of getting selected drop significantly, as it shows a lack of confidence.

Your eyebrows serve more purpose than simply completing your face. Use them to full advantage to show inquisitiveness. You can focus your eyebrows together to signify that you have not understood what has just been said. However, too much of squinting may backfire, as it will be overdoing it. You can show 'surprise' by raising your eyebrows, despite a certain English idiom appointing an entirely different interpretation to 'raising eyebrows.' Express shock or mild surprise by exploiting your eyebrows smartly.

Your facial expressions cover more than just your eyes, lips and eyebrows. It is how your face as a whole is presented that matters and not just its individual parts. When you have a smiling face, it is natural that those sitting right across the interview table feel good vibes coming from you. On the other hand, a face with a grimace on it is considered cold and unfriendly.

Body Postures

Body postures are all about how you carry yourself. It is the ultimate platform for your body language to be displayed in full vigor.

Sitting is as important as walking. Do not pull the chair out and just assume that you are to sit unless someone asks you to. It is not only against your prospects of landing a job, but also rude to sit down on your own as it gives off an aura of superiority. Wait for one of the interviewers to ask you to sit. Assume a straight posture, with your backbone touching the back of the chair at all points. Do not sit too stiff, as that could lead to cramps and make you nervous eventually.

Do not sit slouching. Straighten up your shoulders a bit and appear smart while doing so. Do not cross your legs under the table. Though most interviewers cannot see what is going on under the table, that position does affect your upper body. One can easily tell how casually your legs are placed under the table by taking a single glance at your upper body.

Do not place one leg above the other while sitting. It shows that you are not just confident about yourself, but also show a general attitude of carelessness towards the interviewers. Behave in a manner that sends the message that you respect them.

Sitting upright in an interview might go in favor of you since it displays an attentive mentality. On the other hand, adopting a slouching position signifies that you are in the mood to hear them out and are only there only to doodle and pass time.

Gestures

In an interview, if you are sitting in a cross-armed position, it implies that you are not welcome to others' point of views and ideas. It displays a cold attitude and often does not come off as desirable. On the other hand, instead of crossing arms, if you sit with your hands in your lap or on the table, you give off a friendly and warmer aura and it will definitely fetch you brownie points.

It is a sign of careless confidence to casually fling your arms around while walking. On the other hand, if you clench your fists and walk, it may imply that you are calculated and reserved about yourself.

In certain countries, finger gestures can be interpreted in several ways. The majority of our planet follows the rule of showing the middle finger to be offensive. On the other hand, in some parts of the world, it's the display of index finger that's considered aggressive and offensive.

Hands can be used to convey emotions too. Joining your hands in a Namaste sign shows that you mean respect towards the person. Bowing down is another form of respect followed by the Japanese. If you show someone the 'thumbs up' sign, it means that you are either wishing them good luck or are conveying 'okay' or one of its variants. However, if you do the same in other countries like Iran or Thailand; it can be taken as an equivalent of showing the middle finger in the West.

So, make sure you do not consciously or subconsciously offend your interviewers with your body language or gestures.

Handshakes

A very common way to greet each other is by shaking each other's hand. This has been a tradition since the medieval period. A handshake is supposed to signify greeting, completion, agreement or friendship and calling off of war.

In an interview, the first and only physical interaction you will have with your prospective employer is through the handshake that you perform when you first walk in. The way a person shakes his hand with others says a lot about him. If the handshake is firm, it means the person performing it is confident and is clear about his intentions.

On the other hand, if it's a loose handshake, it displays a lack of self-confidence and casualness. A weak handshake is often taken to be a sign towards half-agreement and not a full nod. Studies over the years have classified handshakes into various categories like the Bone Crusher – squeezing hands too hard, and the Limp Fish-weakly done handshake.

Miscellaneous

Biting your nails is a clear sign of anxiety. Though it is perfectly human to be anxious, remember it is a rat race competition out there. Interviewers will be hunting for people that are not going through their own personal issues already. Hence, it is advisable not to bite your nails and give them a chance to strike your name off the list.

Do not nod or shake your head at the wrong times. In a fit of frenzy and a rush to impress, many candidates fail to even grasp the question and simply nod or shake their head. A nod signifies yes and a mere shaking of head denotes no. If you have fully understood the question and are clear and ready to elucidate, only then must you nod or shake your head. Nodding and shaking of the head also comes under body language and must be sparingly used.

Do not flinch at a question that has caught you unaware. It is perfectly fine for a candidate to come across questions that might baffle them from the very beginning. However, do not make any gesture that says, 'I am not liking this question and I hate you for asking it.'' Instead of flinching or making a face, act curious and tell them that you have no idea regarding the question's answer and would like to know the same.

Tell them that you give up despite trying hard, and ask if they could give you the right answer. Such a gesture puts you in a good light. It shows that you have the thirst for knowledge.

Make sure your feet are positioned properly. Feet that are placed in the direction of the door paint a very sorry picture of a candidate. It indicates that the candidate is not very keen on bagging the job and is sitting there just for the sake of appearing at the job interview. It also shows that you are ready to walk out any moment the interview is over which is obviously not a healthy sign.

Overview

When called for an interview, make yourself presentable. A fat belly becomes presentable when accompanied by a well-fitting and ironed somber professionalism-oriented shirt and the right set of pants. Trim, shave and wash before walking in for the interview. Maintain a good posture and talk in a polite manner.

Confidence can be improved by how you look but don't overdo it. Show them that you are a team person and are willing to take up leadership positions when asked to. If asked something that flips you out, instead of freaking out, stay calm and honestly tell them you have no idea. Do not overdo the way you speak and just talk how you would normally talk with your friends. Impress them with your logical clarity, communication skills and technical know-how that are pre-requisites for the job.

Chapter 4

Common Interview Questions

- How did you learn about this job?

- Why do you want this job?

- What are your biggest strengths?

- What are your biggest weaknesses

- Tell me more about yourself?

- What are you the best fit for this position?

- What are your salary expectations?

- Why did you leave your last job?

- What are you future goals?

- Tell me about an experience where you had to deal with a difficult situation.

- How do you handle failure?

- How do you handle success?

- What makes you stand out from the rest of the applicants?

- Where do you see yourself in 5 years? 10 years?

- What do you look to accomplish in the first 30 days? 90 days?

- Why are you interested in this company specifically?

- What is your greatest motivation in life?

- How do you handle stressful situations?

• Tell me about a time when you disagreed with your boss or manager.

• What do you like the least and the most about this industry?

• What are your favorite hobbies and pastimes?

• Are you more of a leader or a follower? Why?

• Why was there a gap in your employment between [date] and [date]?

• What can you uniquely bring to this company that others can't?

• If money wasn't an option, what would you do with your life?

• How do you handle mistakes? Tell me about a time when you did.

• What is your single-most greatest accomplishment?

- How would go about firing somebody?

- What is your ideal work environment?

- What is your leadership style?

- What is the toughest decision you've had to make in the past 9 months?

- What was your salary in your previous job?

- What are your top three traits?

- What traits would you look for when hiring somebody?

- What are our company values?

- What is our company's highest priority?

- What other companies are you considering?

- Have you been fired before? If so, why?

- How would your previous boss and coworkers describe you?

- If you could be any animal, what would it be?

- What is your favorite website?

- What is your favorite book?
- What is your favorite magazine/journal?

- What makes you the most uncomfortable?

- Are you willing to travel/relocate?

- Would you be willing to work 40+ hours a week?

- Would you be willing to work on holidays?

- What makes you wake up every morning?

- Do you know the name of our CEO?

- If you started your own organization, what would your top 5 values be?

- Are you good or bad at asking for assistance?

- What was your college experience like?

- What were your responsibilities in your last job?

- How do you deal with unresponsive coworkers or clients?

- Tell me about a situation when you were unsure of how to move forward. How did you respond?

- You find yourself working on a project that you cannot complete because your colleague has not submitted their work. How do you respond?

- Do you prefer written or verbal communication?

- What do you do if there is a breakdown of communication on your team?

- What would you do if you saw an employee stealing supplies?

- What would you do if somebody took credit for your ideas?

- How well do you think this interview is going so far?

- Are there any questions that I haven't asked you yet?

- Do you have any questions for me?

Closing Thoughts

Attitude before actions. That is the sequence you must master. The purpose of this book was not simply give you things to do, but give you a vision of who to be. This is the key. This is the secret.

As the opening quote insightfully said, the interview will never rise beyond the person being interviewed. Even if you can say all the "right" answers, parrot the correct responses, and look the part, if your demeanor and aura does not exhibit the confidence the world looks for, you will always be at the mercy of the interviewers.

Remember, life is full of interviewers. But never submit yourself to the system. Never submit yourself to simply vying for the approval of the next big person. Be the next big person, and the rest will follow.

Yours,
Henry.

Review this book!
Change link to book review after publishing

Free Books on

Success and Productivity

Hey! If you're interested in reviewing some free books on business, leadership, success, and productivity (including getting our next published eBook free for review)

Then visit this link here: http://eepurl.com/cS1_BT

Leave a Review

If you found this short book was helpful at all or provided even a small insight that you took away, would you consider helping other people find this book by leaving this book an honest review? That'd mean a lot!

About the Author

Henry lives in Manhattan and is happily married to the love of his life Lily. He has three kids, Sammie, Hillary, and Jeff, all of whom went to Yale--Henry's alma meter. Henry got his undergraduate degrees in both Marketing and Finance at the New York University before finishing his MBA at Yale. Henry is a speaking consultant, fitness enthusiast, and tea drinker. He also loves watching the NBA and How I Met Your Mother.

Recommended Resources:

- How to Win Friends & Influence People – Dale Carnegie

- How to Answer Interview Questions – Peggy McGee

- Secrets of Power Negotiating – Roger Dawson

- Think and Grow Rich – Napoleon Hill

- How Success People Think – John C. Maxwell

- Influence: The Psychology of Persuasion – Robert Cialdini

• Copyright

• © 2017 Henry F. Santiago

- First Edition

End